Kissing catastrophe

Jenna Malin

a poem a day
keeps the pain at bay.
at least, it's supposed to.
six books later, *I still miss you.*

For permissions, contact:

info.jennasdilemmas@gmail.com

ISBN: 979-8-9868209-4-1

To all the catastrophes out there like me: you are *so worthy* of love, even when you can't always see it. Somehow, someday, *you will*.

TABLE OF CONTENTS

ACKNOWLEDGEMENTS

To everyone who volunteered their time to be on my ARC team for this book. You know who you are, and I'm so grateful for you.

To my husband, my biggest fan, the love of my life, Tom. Every love poem I have and ever will write, I write with *you* in mind. (*Especially* the spicy ones.)

Part One:

the Kiss

jenna malin

we were broken by design—
meant to be made whole
only by *coming together*.

soulmates.
two halves of
the same heartache.
only made better by

      the promise of forever.

I ache to hold his heart.
we are one soul, p u l l e d   a p a r t.

    but I know, in time,
        his heart will be mine.

however long it takes, *I will wait for you.*
I will hold my breath until I turn blue.
I will suffocate before I forsake you.

I'd like to think you'd do the same.

I put my heart
on the line
for you.
I hung it out to dry
with the very
best of them.
clothes-pinned
to the twine,
it beats only for
you and I.

it will wait
    for you until
        the end of time.

if you think
you're falling
in love with me,

            s t o p.

I am *not*
the girl of
your dreams.
I am the stuff of

        n i g h t m a r e s.

you will fall
from grace
     down
         down
            d o w n
and wake up
moments before
you hit the ground.

if you think
you're falling
in love with me,

            d o n ' t.

…or, do.
because I can't help
but fall in love
with you.

don't follow me down
unless you're ready to drown.
don't take my hand
unless you understand

I am not safe or sound.

I want to show you what it's like
to live inside my mind, but I fear
it is not safe for you here.
it is uncharted, treacherous territory
    haunted by all the ghosts I've loved before,

                and I don't need another love to mourn.

I lie awake wondering if
loving me is a waste
of your time.

I lie awake wondering if
I could love you
into loving me
anyway.

I was broken when I met you.
heart littered with ragged scars,
my cheeks tear-stained, with frown lines
that stretched on for miles.

when I first met you, I knew
that *this time would be different.*
that *this love would be magnificent*
if I only would let you in.

I was broken when I met you,
but now I am whole.

> *I knew I wouldn't regret you.*

the night we met, the last thing
I expected to do was fall for you.
I wasn't looking, but *there you were.*
my one and only. my north star.
the other half of my broken heart.
it didn't know wholeness until you
held it in your gentle hands.

I never knew love could feel like that:
like *coming home.* like *becoming whole.*
like my soul being sewn together
after eons of feeling afraid and alone.

the night we met, the last thing
I expected to do was fall for you.
it was as if my heart knew you would
always be there to catch me,
and *there you are.*

on your knees, promising me forever
with the same hands that put me back together.
with the same lips that have never left mine wanting.
with the same heart that has loved me
more than I ever thought possible.

I never knew love could feel like that:
like *a perfect match.*

I have fallen for you.
so incredibly hard,
so unbelievably fast.
the depths of my heart
have grown so vast,
no one else's heart could ever fill
the chasm I carved in mine
to fit yours safely inside.
yours, and yours *alone.*

I have fallen for you,
and made my heart your home.

please come home.

you must think I'm crazy
for loving someone so
painfully different
than me.

but when I look at him,
all I see is someone sweet
to tame my bitter taste,
someone so perfect
for me in every way.

when I look at him, all I see
is someone so amazing.

just... *look at him.*

can you blame me?

people wait eternities,
wish upon infinities
for the love standing
right in front of me.

people dream of epiphanies,
pray to their divinities for
the love you give to me.

I have waited *for* you,
    and I have dreamed *of* you.

and here you are:
living, breathing, and
fulfilling *every*
                single
                        one.

you are a broken dream,
a healthy heart
beating too
hard and
vast.

I don't know
if we will
last,

but here I am:

f
  a
   l
    l
     i
      n
       g fast.

each time you fall in love,
you're giving someone
a little piece of yourself
to have and to hold
with the promise
to do so *carefully*.

"caution: fragile heart enclosed.
will replace if broken."

I keep a piece of your heart
locked in my bedside drawer.
not a locker, not a safe,
because I swore to keep it close
no matter how far you go.

close enough that
I can always hear it say,

"I will always
    beat for you.
        only you.

        only always."

I will keep your heart safe.
keep it warm, loved.
I will hold it close,
and I will *never*
let it go.

please, don't let me go.

I love in absolutes—tidal waves.
full speed ahead, no breaks.
I love with my whole heart or not at all.
I don't just *love*.
I f
a
l
l.

I'm f
    a
     l
      l
       i
        n
         g again, full speed ahead with no brakes.

I'm f
    a
     l
      l
       i
        n
         g again, and *heartbreak awaits*.

I will do whatever it takes to be loved by you.
if only for a moment. *if only for a lifetime.*
I'll do whatever it takes to make you *mine*.

when we get like this,
it's easy to understand why
love and *us* can't coexist.

we are two opposing forces:
the push and the pulling away.
the giving and taking too much.
the severing of trust and the spilling of blood;
acts unforgivable, unworthy of acquittal.
we are two brittle hearts and four clenched fists.
love is not supposed to hurt like this.

so, I know *love* and *us* can't coexist.
at least, we shouldn't.
but, we do.

I simply can't exist without you.

when we get like this,
it's very clear we don't mix.

like oil and water,
we toil and swim harder,
desperate to make it work.

    but we won't.

despite our best efforts
to keep our love afloat,
I'm fully prepared

                to drown.

break down the walls around my heart.
love me in the depths of all my shadows.
pull me into shallow waters—teach me how to swim.
take me by the hand—*teach me how to love again.*

my heart is a mess.
it's an ocean of secrets,
and I don't know how to swim.

I've spent my life treading water,
dreading the day my limbs will give out
and my lungs will gasp for breath
and I'll choke on water instead.

but loving you…
it's like beaching for the first time.
like finally reaching shore and finding
there's something more than this loveless life.

like warm sand on soft skin.
palm trees dancing in the salty, light breeze
while the tide rolls in and washes away
every secret I've ever buried deep in the sand.

my heart is a mess.
but then you take my hand,
and I'm in heaven on land.

your eyes are so enticing;
oblivion *so inviting.*

like crystal clear pools
filled to the brim with
your every cruel whim.

I could drown in you.

all s
    i
      n
        k,

           no swim.

love is like quicksand.
the harder you fight it,
the tighter it clings.

the faster you swim,
the deeper you s

                  i

                  n

                  k.

relationships evolve, change.
some dissolve, f a   d   e.

but our love will defy
the sands of time.

you drag
me deeper into
you with every sigh.
I long to be the breath
you catch in your
throat, the love
you never
want to let go
of. I am so
close to giving in
to the ache, the
way you take
me into
your heart,
break mine
apart.
if there is
anything left
to break, *you* of
all people have
the honor.
you of
all
the stars
in the world
combined have
the power to
realign my
missing
pieces.
you
of all
have the
power to
call me
home.

you are my
north
star, my
guiding light.
you shine bright
into my eyes,
but, even
blinded,
I will
find
us.
across
time and
space, I will
climb the whole
way on my hands
and knees. no
cosmic mountain
could keep us apart.
even with my
eyes closed,
my heart
always
knows
where you
are. it is the
only map I need;
a compass that
only leads me
to you.
wherever
you may be,
you will
never
be
far from
me.

I am so far gone for you—
so recklessly
  irrevocably
    incessantly
      gone.

some would say lost—
hopelessly
  terrifyingly
    impossibly
      lost.

but they don't know what I know—
that *you* are my compass.
my map. my northern star.
the sun my world
spins around.

you will *never* be far from me.
no matter how far I roam,
you are the lighthouse
that will always
lead me
home.

you are my truth. my northern star.
my whole universe spins around *us*.
whenever I miss you,
all I have to do
is look up.

the stars in me
shine far beneath
the surface of my skin.

beneath my heart
beating hard
and bright within.

glowing now,
forever moonlit.

I told the stars about him.
I wished on them, and they
whispered back to me,

"you deserve better than him."

then, they sent me you.
and when we finally kissed,

they aligned.

the stars that aligned
and pulled you into
my life are the only things
that hold me together
during my darkest nights.

you are my cosmic destiny.
my fate *divine.*

I can't see the forest
through the trees.
the wilderness
could breathe
me back to life,
but all I see tonight are
all the stars aligning
and leading me

home to you.

I'm what some may call *a controlled burn*.
smoldering embers yearning to blaze.
flickering flames chained to a fireplace.
stoked by the heat of your breath
tickling my neck, your moans on my skin.
your kiss ignites a spark in me,
unearths my heart buried beneath
mountains of ash and soil
and sends it *soaring*.

like a phoenix *roaring to life*.

I spend my days
dreaming about the way
you undress me with your eyes,
burning with desire—

your love is an unquenchable fire.

I have been burned so many times,
but I am not afraid of the flames
flickering in your eyes.
all it takes is one kiss,
one taste of your lips, and

I'm ready to burn alive.

metaphors to describe my heart:

(after Amy Kay)

1.) an overstuffed suitcase—filled to the brim with all the love I have to give.
2.) a ticking time bomb—counting down the days until I see your face again.
3.) a centuries-old bridge—watch your step, lest you fall for me like all the rest.
4.) a storm cloud—after decades of drought.
5.) a loaded gun, taking aim—*Cupid made some upgrades.*
6.) an empty grave—with room for two.
7.) a photo album—*I only keep pictures of you.*

if I gave you my heart,
would be strong enough to hold it?
would you crumple beneath its weight,
or would *you*, unfamiliar with your own strength,
crush it?

> if I gave you my heart,
>> *would you know how to love it?*

hold me like a secret.
keep me like an oath.
seal me with a kiss.

don't let me go.

kiss my hand and make me well.
keep my secrets, never tell.
never make me say

farewell.

my heart is beating at warped speed,
fluttering fast like hummingbird wings.
I never thought someone would catch me.

but here I am, like putty in your hands.
please, be careful with me.

when you look me in the eyes, I swear *I could fly*.
I could sprout wings with the way
your smile sends my heart fluttering.

I swear I could soar with the way
your touch leaves me aching for more.
with the way your lips on my skin
love me *just right*, leave me
moaning through the night.

words cannot describe the intoxicating high
that floods through my body when
you quiet the demons inside me.
you quell their thirst with romantic words
and seductions *so exciting*.

when you look me in the eyes,
I swear I could spend
a lifetime by
your side.

I have loved you for a lifetime.
and in the blink of an eye,
you will be mine, our hearts
forever intertwined.

I have loved you through high and low.
and I know my love will only grow,
shimmer in the night sky like
the brightest moonstone.

I have loved you the hardest I can,
held your hand through
the darkness to help you stand.

I have loved you in ways
I'll never fully understand.
the depths of my heart were
unchartered waters before you made land.

I have loved you with my whole body.
every fiber, string, every little atomic thing
holding me together.

I have loved you from the start.
and I *will* love you with my whole heart,
through every night, through
every part, dark and light.

I will love you all my life.

I cross my heart and hope to die
and spend my afterlife
with your hand in mine.
six feet deep, side by side,
I'll be yours until the end of time…

if you'll have me.
if you'll be mine.

you trapped me in your heart,
and I trapped you in poetry,
so our love will live on
long after we're both
dead and gone.

the elusive blue sky is overcast and humid.
the tears in my eyes rain down on the ruins
where we laid down our hearts, their roots
sewn into one another—*intertwined.*

we are so at home in contaminated soil,
acid rain could never wash away
what our love already diluted—
this impossible dream that

      you could love someone so wounded.

I don't have much,
  but I still have your love.

        and that's *more* than enough.

you are my muse.　　*without you, the world would not know of art.*
you are my air.　　*my reason to breathe when my chest feels heavy.*
you are my heart.　　*without you, it would cease completely.*
the sparkle in my eye.　*my sunrise, the light at the end of my tunnel.*
laughter caught in my mouth.　*without you, I would never smile.*
shivers rippling across my skin.　*every tantalizing touch does me in.*

you are my everything.　　*and without you, I would feel nothing.*

no matter how hard I try,
I will never be able to look at you
and pretend I feel nothing.
with you, I feel *everything*.

you smile at me, and
every atom comes alive.
electrified by your touch,
amplified with every brushstroke
of your lips against my throat.

you seize my hand and
every pore expands to inhale
your presence while they can
and they can never get enough.

you drag your fingers along my thigh,
deliberate paths d
                    o
                     w
                        n and back with a euphoric sigh.

                        loving you makes me feel *so alive.*

when I'm with you, I feel alive again.
every atom *electrified* by the sound of your voice.
the most beautiful noise I've ever heard
is my name on your lips.
your kiss is a whispered promise:

I will love you until the sun loses its shine.
I will love you for the rest of my life.

you pull me close and whisper in my ear
everything I've been dying to hear:
my name, *a moan on your lips.*

I bite down on mine to keep yours from escaping.
I love the way it tastes in my mouth.

> *I don't know how I've ever been without.*

I want to choke on your words,
to drink the promises directly from your lips.
I want to be drunk on your kiss,
to writhe under the stroke
of your fervent fingertips.

yes, yes, love me *just like this*.

I find a little piece of heaven
    in every love letter you send.

I worship your words;
    the most addictive sounds I've ever heard.

you're so pretty
when you lie to me.
the way those words
spill so effortlessly
off those lips
I'm *dying* to kiss
is so addictive,
you leave me
delirious with
restraint.

I don't care
what else you say
as long as one of those
     blasphemous words is

my name.

when you look in my eyes,
don't be surprised to see yourself in them.
you are all I think about—the *only* thing on my mind.

when it comes to love,
there's only you and I.

devour *me*—not my body.
    kiss my *soul*—not my lips.
        touch my *heart*—not my skin.

    don't tell me
        that you love me—

            show me.

tell me you love me
without *telling me* you love me.

hold my hand during a horror movie.
hear my laughter from across the room and smile.
search for me in a sea of a thousand people
and do not rest until you are next to me.
on the couch, pull my legs over your lap
and hold them close to your chest.
trace delicate patterns along my skin
like goosebumps are your favorite art form.
hold my face when you kiss me, *and don't let go.*

that way, when you tell me you love me, *I'll already know.*

I want to know what love is.
so, I look into your eyes—
your hazel irises are
perfection *divine.*

I look inside your heart
and I see mine, full and kind.
I look at your hands,
trembling as you reach up
brush my cheek with your thumb
leave behind a rosy blush
and I smile.

I want to know what love is.
so, I open my heart
and invite you in.

I opened my heart to you—
a desolate place with crumbling walls
and ghosts haunting its empty halls.
I opened my heart to you knowing
the probability of you—of *us*—exorcizing
the demons that reside in its darkest corners and
building a home safe for holy souls: *slim to none.*

but I opened my heart to you hoping
that you would prove me wrong;
that, *no*, not all lovers are monsters,
and, *no*, not all monsters have teeth.
that some have hearts just like mine:
desperate to trust and be loved by another,
gaping and waiting to be occupied.

I opened my heart to you—
won't you come inside?

my heartsong is incomplete
without yours keeping time
with mine like a drumbeat.

I love you

    thump-thump

  I need you

      thump-thump

    I will never leave you

        thump-thump

there is no one else for me.
you are the only one I will ever need.

I'll be the first to admit it: I'm blinded by your lips.
struck dumb by your kiss. speechless. weightless.
floating through the air—unfurled—not a care
in the world—*but you.*

however, I'll be the first to admit
I'm not equipped to love you the way you deserve.
maybe because of my injured self-worth
or the damage left by those
who came before you.

I wish I could say you were my first,
but I'll be the first to admit it—*you weren't.*
I wanted you to be. oh, *so* badly,
because I knew we were meant to be
the moment you laid eyes on me.
but this heart had been previously occupied.
or, more accurately—invaded—raided—*desecrated.*

I'll be the first to admit it:
sometimes, when I'm with you, I'm not.
my body may be, but my thoughts are far away.
my soul, betrayed—isolated—*devastated.*

but… I'll be the first to admit it:
when I *am* with you—and I mean *really* with you—
I catch a glimpse of what it's like to be free.

let me be the one to free you, too.

it's hard to be what you need
when you never talk to me.
tell me that you need me,
want to be next to me

for all eternity.

that's all I'm asking for—
a promise that you will love me more
than the life you had before,
even when it seems impossible.

make loving me feel possible.

I arrive at your doorstep—your chest—a hair's breadth
from your lips, and I peer into your windows—your eyes—
but the curtains are drawn. the lights are off.
you've left a note on the door:
there's no one home.

but… I can *feel* you.
lying on your bedroom floor, curled up, *writhing.*
barely surviving all the pain you keep buried
deep inside this home you've
made out of heartache.

    unlock the door, invite me in.
        I promise, *you will never be alone again.*

open your heart and
show me who you are.
I am *desperate* to know you
down to the root, the core, the bone.

I am *destined* to show you

you are not alone.

you are not alone in this.

    please, *let me hold your brokenness.*

I don't want your body,
I want to know *your soul.*
let me take you by the hand
*and let me make you
whole again.*

unzip me and crawl inside—*wear me like armor.*
part me down the middle—*split me with honor.*

if you are going to make me your martyr,
then please—*love me harder.*

and if I dare
to love you back—

       I will be a goner.

I almost can't believe that someone
like you could love someone like me:
so broken and battle-scarred.
warped and bent in all the wrong places.

I've mended myself so many times,
I don't know if the person you fell for
is the *real* me or someone different completely.
if *she* is who I was meant to be all along—
the one destined for you—or if the woman
I once was is still inside of me somewhere,
cocooned and waiting for her moment
to emerge, to bloom—*to be perfect for you.*

I almost can't believe that regardless of what I think,
there's not a single thing you'd change about me.
that you love me as I am and not as I could be,
or what I think I *should* be.
that you undress me down to my soul
and *still* see someone beautiful.
someone worthy.

      someone enough.

I almost can't believe
that I deserve
your love…

      almost.

for the longest time,
I wanted to change myself
into someone you could love.
I never thought I could become her:
the girl you love. *a complete stranger.*

I don't even recognize her
staring at me in the mirror.
I see faint glimpse of the old me:
my nose, my lips, chapped, bitten.
but I've recently discovered,
you don't love *her*—
you love *me*.

you love my every blemish and scar,
cherish every dark corner of my heart
in ways I never could; *in all the ways I know I should.*

you kiss away my charade,
all the pain written on my skin.
and, what's even more amazing is, *I let you.*
your love is unbidden, but *so very welcome.*

> with you, all my sins
>   are forgiven—*every single one.*

all the hopeless places I've found love:

1.) at Costco—by the wine boat, before the coffins.
2.) at the Goodwill down the street—in the twenty-five cent bins.
3.) in his arms—*where I was meant to be.*
4.) the roller-skating rink—where I skinned my knees.
5.) the trunk of my car—where my spare tire should be.
6.) within myself—*you unearth it in me.*

we met in a warzone—both fighting battles invisible to the naked eye. our war cries falling on deaf ears. our tears spilling faster than the blood from our self-inflicted wounds. I didn't know who I was before you—a soldier lost to shellshock. frozen like stone. oblivious to every grenade thrown in my direction, every bullet hurtling toward my head.

we united in the trenches—drenched in layers of mud mixed with our own blood. transfixed by every explosion, entranced by the notion that we might not make it through the night. but when you gripped my hand, suddenly, *I could breathe again.* you tethered my soul to my body, brought me back to the here and now where nothing matters but *you and I.* nothing but making it out alive *with you by my side.*

when we met, I was the victim of every man that came before you. of every meal and every pound, every ounce of regret spinning like a carousel in my head. *when we met, I was dizzy with regret.* and you, the victim of every woman I'll never know. of every dark alley and ominous shadow. every needle and pill, every spilled drink. *when we met, we were both on the brink.*

and when you and I collided, the universe sighed with relief. the battle was already won.

together, *we are free to run.*

loving you is my favorite form of self-destruction.
the more I love you, the more I break.
the faster I fall, the quicker I s h a   t   t   e   r.

and each time I pull myself to my feet,
you are there to pull me back to my knees
and into your arms where you *swear* I'll be safe.

the more you lie, the more I believe you.
the harder you cling, the less I want to leave.
because without you, I have nothing left to lose,

and if love is war, *you are my weapon of choosing.*

love is war, and *you don't fight fair*.

love is a blood sport played
by those unafraid to put their hearts on display;
to wear them on careless sleeves and see
just how brutal love can be.

love is a blood sport played
by those unashamed of being flayed open,
laid bare, of begging, *kiss me here, touch me there.*
blissfully unaware of the war being waged
on the body, of the damage being done
by the ones who swore to love it.

love is a blood sport played
by those chained to the belief that
someone who loves you would *never*
be the one to hurt you; slaves to delusion
betrayed beyond absolution.

love is a blood sport
    I know I'll never win.

but for you, *I play.*

kissing catastrophe

plunge your blade deep into me.
make my heart your sheath
and *lay waste to me.*

waste one more wish on me.
    make me your wildest fantasy.

let the ball drop, time stop,
kiss me nonstop until
the sun comes up.

desire unfurled, *take me.*
    if I am to be your world, *waste me.*

ruin me for anyone else.
    just for tonight—*let's rebel.*

you can love me,
but this, I warn you:
you can touch me, want me,
lie and say that you love me,
but the moment you do,

I will never unlove you.

caress my heart,
beating hard against
the cage holding it in place,
preventing its inevitable escape.

pry the bars apart
and free me from this fate.

seize my heart—
it's yours to claim.

sink your teeth into my flesh,
devour me until there's *nothing left.*

I am yours. *all yours.*
    what are you *waiting for?*

I don't know when you sunk your teeth in me,
but I know I am ready to succumb,
surrender at the mercy of your tongue
speaking a language known only by the two of us.
our pulses racing, hearts in sync,

I always knew loving you would be the death of me.

let's devour each other in a passionate frenzy.
kiss me—touch me—love me—*everywhere.*
send my heart reeling into some kind of feeling,
falling—screaming—gasping—*careening.*
hold me tight, pull me close—close—*so close.*

tonight, I am yours—yours—*all yours.*

I dreamt I drank the color of your voice—
red velvet sugarcoating my tongue
with sweet nothings.

you whisper hushed, decadent confessions
in my ear, and I drink them in,
sink into my glass, my crimson lipstick
printed on the rim of yours.

your moans carry me well into the morning—
cherry and grenadine, sickeningly sweet,
but my wildest dreams are *nothing*
compared to your lips on me.

with my lips
  against the rim
    of my mug,
I take slow sips
   of our love and
     hold them under
       my tongue.

        I only ever want to consume *us*.

I savor you with every swallow.
I pull you in, drink your lips,
inhale your kiss.

I never thought love could be *so delicious*.

kissing catastrophe

you brush your lips,
featherlight kiss, against mine
and watch me come u n   d   o   n   e.

I take one look deep into your eyes
and I know the worst
is yet to come.

I ache to sink into the bliss
of those tantalizing fingertips
that traverse the curves of my body
you've already mapped with your tongue.

with one taste of your indulgent lips, *I come undone.*

loving you is like tasting forbidden fruit.
I shouldn't want to sink my teeth into you, *but I do*.

one taste is all it takes to *devour you*.

I'll do what I must
to satisfy this lust.
to satiate this hunger,
quiet this thunder
pounding in my chest.

put your lips on mine.

I'll handle the rest.

I crave you like the sun after years spent in darkness.
like warmth on my skin after eons spent shivering.
your fingertips leave goosebumps in their wake
as they caress my face and I *ache* for more.

and when your lips find mine, *I am insatiable.*

lure me to the edge
and pull me right back.
free my body from its clothes
and touch me *just like that.*

love me.
all of me.
that's all I ask.

when the lights are off,
and your inhibitions
have come and gone,
let the world fall away,
and stay with me.

slip between these
passion-soaked sheets
and sink into the moment,
become one with
the need.

let me be the one you need.

we are a labyrinth of entwined limbs
and tangled sheets, hearts beating
to the rhythm of needing more.
I need more.
      more.
        more.

treat my body like a maze—
discover me for the rest of our days.

if the heart is a muscle,
and muscles have memory,
then that must mean mine
has the rhythm of yours
memorized.

if you undress me, will you caress me?
will you handle me with care?
kiss me *here*, touch me *there?*
will you treasure my body bare?

if I let you into my heart,
will you promise to fill it wholly?
to chase out the darkness making a home of me?
will you cherish it—my heart—as something holy?

if I show you my broken,
will you heal me—nurse me back to health?
will you be the one to put me first
and break this excruciating curse?

if I show you where it hurts,
will you have me at my worst?

on nights like these,
I feel like the queen of catastrophe.
a broken shell of the beautiful girl I used to be
before you came along—you made me *complete*.

on nights like these,
I feel like the ghost of a girl who learned
she was not loved the way she deserved.
not until you came along and showed her
where she belonged—*in your arms*.

on nights like these,
I am *writhing* in my sheets, tossing and turning
waking and worrying that I will look over
and you'll have left me like all the rest—
an inconsolable, unmitigated *mess*.

on nights like these,
you love me the best.

it doesn't take an artist to see
what we have is *a masterpiece*.
lovers fated by design.

>   *your catastrophic heart was made for mine.*

when you take me in your hands,
can you feel the misery amassed in my skin?
all my atoms are filled to the brim
and on the brink of collapse.
can you feel the carnage left behind
by every man who came before you?
every scar and divot, every stitch healed over
and buried so deeply, I truly believe
they're the only thing holding me together.
when you take me in your hands, *do you feel that?*

or, when you take me in your hands,
are you filling all my emptiness with your wholeness?
mending every fracture, filling every crevice with gold,
transforming me into something precious to behold?
are you healing all my festering wounds
with your tender heart and gentle palms?
when you take me in your hands,
can you feel me—the real me—*healing bones and all?*

yes, I can, you mumble into my hair
as I melt into your haven arms,
and it is safe for you to fall.

when you kiss me,
can you taste the pain on my tongue?
the metallic tang of my atrophied heart, riddled
with scars left behind by everyone who swore
they would love me for the rest of their life—*and lied?*
can you taste every second I ever wasted
on loving everyone who isn't you?
can you taste the name of the person who
turned loving me into blasphemy?
when you kiss me, *do you taste catastrophe?*

or, when you kiss me,
do you do so with fervor and wonder,
who on Earth would ever want to hurt her?
do you taste the alchemy catalyzed by
the collision of our lips—our souls—our bodies
becoming whole beneath a blanket of stars
and a cacophony of blissful moans
that make God himself blush?
how can you kiss me when you know
you're kissing catastrophe?

no, you declare into my trembling skin.
you whisper to me, lips dripping sincerity,
I'm making love to a masterpiece.

you see me—*the real me.*
you love me—*the good, bad, and ugly.*
you undress me down to the soul,
chase away all my shadows,
and you still find me *beautiful.*

I never knew love could be *so simple.*

it's the beginning that hurts.
like the pinprick of a needle plunging into the skin.
you know it will be worth it,
that the benefits will far outweigh
the fleeting discomfort of the pain
and serve a greater purpose.
but, still, you flinch.

it's the beginning that hurts.
that kismet moment where two hearts collide
at the speed of light and burst into stardust;
a kaleidoscopic whirlwind of passion and lust
and you are just along for the ride
because you took one look into
their star-crossed eyes and knew
you would love them
for a lifetime.

it's the beginning that hurts.
because you know that every
    starting point meets a finish line,
        every morning wanes into night,

                and every *hello* ends with *goodbye.*

jenna malin

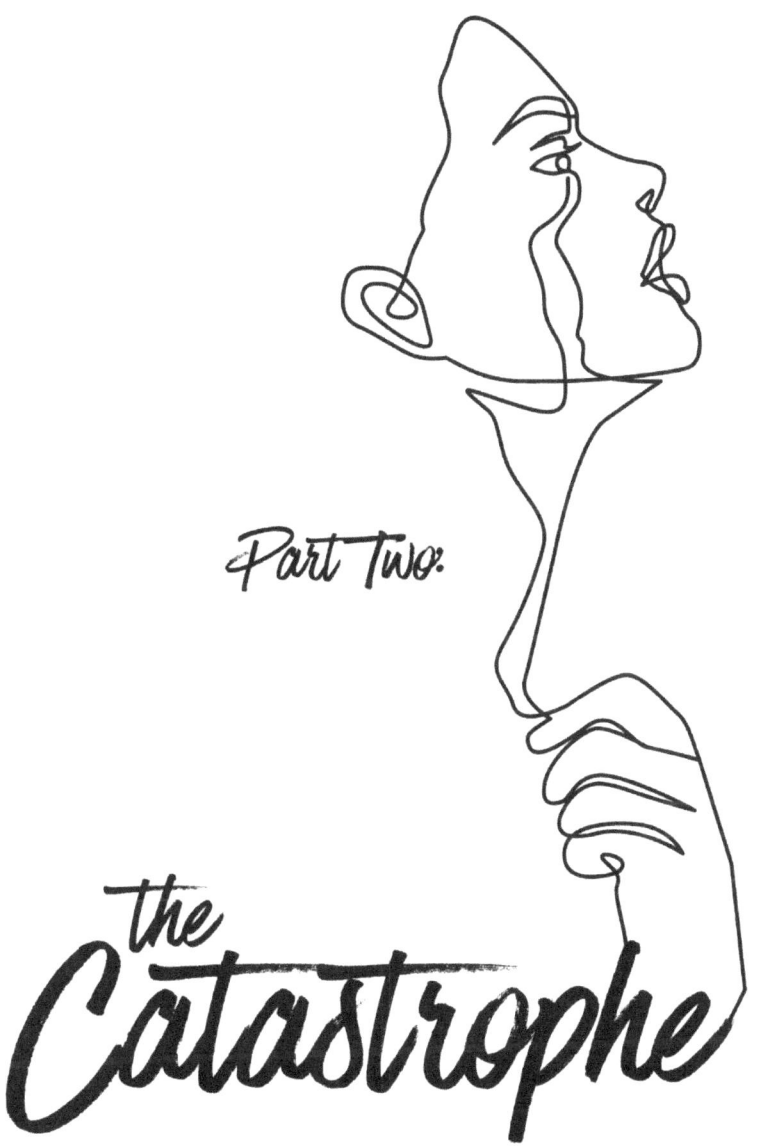

Part Two:

the Catastrophe

jenna malin

my heart in your fist,
you spin a tale I can't resist:

boy meets girl,
becomes her whole world, then

$$s \ h \quad a \quad t \quad t \quad e \quad r \quad s \ it.$$

the scars on my heart tell the story of *us*.
a braille-written, pain-ridden tale of
loving and hating, of falling and breaking.
they say *love is blind*, and here I find myself
with my eyes closed, feeling you everywhere I go.

they say *love is blind*, and they're right.
when you said *I love you*, you lied.

it fools me every time.

I love
without regrets.
with no holds barred,
I have always loved *hard*.

I loved you
with all my heart…
and you left it
b-r-o-k-e-n
and
scarred.

I think we were cursed from the start,
destined to b-r-e-a-k each other's hearts.

   I knew the moment
     I met you we would
            tear
              each
                other
                  a p a   r   t.

our hearts are wound together by fate
and bound by their valves to break.

something inside of me always knew
that letting myself fall for you
would be *my worst mistake.*

you must have mistaken me for someone else—
someone you were meant to love.

because deep in my heart,
I have always known it wasn't me,
and maybe that's what made this so hard—
knowing my heart was just a placeholder,
and wanting you to hold it anyway.

it has taken far too long
for me to learn that *you*
are not the one I was
destined to love.

that I was destined to meet you,
desperate to need you,
but meant to
leave you.

it's so hard for me to believe
that you and I were
not meant to be.

this is how I was left:
cold, empty, *gasping for breath*.
I can see where your fingers
were clamped around my neck,
bruised—used—*neglected*.
my voice, silenced. muted.
no one around to dispute
the lies you spewed *so recklessly*.
before you, I never viewed myself
with such disdain. *as such a mess*.

this is how I was left:
a ruinous wreck.

we walked into this
with no expectations.
this being *insatiable lust.*
this being *infallible trust.*
this being *indelible love.*

you were the *last* person I expected to fall for…
and the last person I expected to *leave.*

I can't keep pretending that we never happened.
that I don't wait at the window for you every night
with the front door ajar, wondering where you are.
that I don't gaze up at the stars, mouth agape,
a gaping hole of ache that echoes
with the sound of your name
whispered alongside three little words
you were too afraid to whisper back.

I can't keep pretending that I don't lick my lips
in a desperate attempt to taste you one last time.
that my heart doesn't beat in sync with yours
in spite of the thousands of miles separating them.
that this heart of mine doesn't feel right
without yours close by to keep it company.
that I don't wish we'd never crossed that line—
that we never had to say *goodbye*.

I can't keep pretending that I don't miss you.
that I don't miss the way our fingers intertwined *so perfectly*.
the way that sparkle in your eyes sent me
floating through time in slow motion.
the way I'd fall for you and, arms outstretched,
open wide, you would catch me *every time*.
I trusted you most of all;
loved you more
than *anything*.

and I can't keep pretending
that you were never
my everything.

I still remember the shape of the sunlight
when you looked me in the eyes and
promised me *our love would never die.*

I still remember the way it bent and reflected
off our skin, illuminating the truth buried deep within
our hearts that both of us already knew,
but refused to believe:

> time was never our friend,
> and *everyone leaves in the end.*

there's a you-shaped
hole in my chest
you made when you left.
you fled my heart so fast,
and you never looked back.

looking back is all I do.

I will always look back for you.

I always thought you would change.
always believed that, eventually,
you would see the error in your ways
and decide to make amends.
that, eventually, you would extend
an olive branch with your apologies
etched in the green.

  but the only thing that changed was my perspective.
    and the only thing that I believe is that *everyone leaves*.

the sun set on us long before
I was ready to fall asleep.

now, I lie awake
in the bed we made love in
before you left that morning,
never to grace my sheets again.

now, the sun has set,
but I won't rest
until we meet
again.

all I wanted
was an answer.
a reason why you
didn't even say
goodbye.

tell me—
how do you
sleep at
night?

       I don't.

most nights, I can't sleep.
    but when I do, *I dream of you.*

I lie down, enveloped by
  the memory of your touch,
    missing your love, because

enough was never enough for me.

I lie awake every night wondering
if loving me was a waste of your time.
if you really loved me, you would still be here
holding me tight.

I lie awake every night because
lying in bed without you
never feels right.

I'm lying awake
making demons of men
and monsters of memories.
convincing myself it's my fault
for confiding in someone who knows
    not of *love*, but only of *want*.
        not of *trust*, but only of *lust*.

I'm lying awake,
writhing in second-hand disgust.

    I should've known not to give you
        my heart if I didn't want it *crushed*.

there is a
  madness in me.
    a secret *unravelling*.
a whisper in
  the white noise.
    an echo in the void.
an inkling.
  a primal instinct.
    a guttural growling.
a monster howling.
      a lover, leaving.
        a heart, *grieving*.

there's a storm brewing. *a turbulent undoing.*
the clouds are swirling, disaster unfurling.
tornadoes are travelling, my sanity unravelling
in the blink of an eye.

funneling. tunneling. *forever struggling.*

what will it take to make
this dark and stormy soul
feel calm and whole again?

what will it take to break this fever,
to pull me back into the ether
where I can become one
with the sun again?

what will it take for me
to learn how to love again?

all the nights I've spent
riddled with regret
tossing and turning
with nothing but worry
spinning in my head
are infinite.

my hurting, tremendous.
my yearning,
worsening.
endless.

when I close
my eyes at night,
I can see more clearly
where you and I meet.

palm to palm, cheek to cheek.
you see right through me,

and I see you leaving.

I have never asked for much.
I've always been easy to love.
easy to please.

and apparently,

      even easier to leave.

I never thought love
    could be so far out of reach.

I never thought my love could leave.

what else is there to say?
you swore you'd never leave,
yet here I lie, left.

my heart heavy, bereft.
my hope, *crushed.*

      here I lie,
           left, and
                  unloved.

HOW DO I GET RID OF YOU?
(after Anna Eisch, *"Rid of You"*)

step one:

> gargle mouthwash and spit you out.
> *repeat until every lover who comes after you is tasteless.*

step two:

> ~~throw up~~ throw out everything you ever gave me.
> *which was everything but your heart.*

step three:

> set it all on fire in the backyard.
> *use all the tears I've shed over you for accelerant.*

step four:

> bottle everything up inside.
> *in all the wine bottles I've emptied since you left.*

step five:

> cut off all my hair
> *to forget how good it felt when you ran your fingers through it.*

step six:

> disappear.
> *ghost myself, just like you did.*

on days like this,
you make me wish I could disappear.
my skin crawls, my heart aches,
and I hate the way it feels.

if I could slip out of my skin
with the same fervor you slithered
your way into it, *I would.*

if I could shrink myself down
to an infinitesimal size, too small to
be observed by the naked eye, *I would.*

on days like this, if I could blink
and never think about you again, *I would.*
because each time you cross
my mind, I feel a little smaller.
I grow a touch weaker.

I never used to hate
myself this much.
not until *you* came along,
    you treacherous creature.

deceiver, deceiver.

only *you* could make
me yearn for the heat of
fire against my skin.

only *you* could make
me long for a love
that *burns*.

only *you* could make
the sting of a blade
in my back feel
so heavenly.

only *you* could make
a lover out of
an enemy.

you
watched me
   hate me and you
        let it *break me.*

you
watched
   me love you
       and left me
           wanting you.

kissing catastrophe

I guess it's fun for you:
breaking me,
saving me,
then taking just enough
to leave me half empty
and begging for
your love.

you were nothing but a bystander—
watching me melt under everything I felt.
watching me get matchstick thin,
inhaling smoke so thick
it made me *sick*.

you watched me suffer
and let me wonder what I did
to deserve to hurt like this.

your silence was *deafening*.
    if only I had been *listening*.

it's been a while since
    I've heard from you.

       your silence speaks volumes.

I should've
known better than
to let the darkness get so close.
only the gravitational pull of the abyss
could make me feel like this:
like a burden *no one would miss.*

like I could scream in a crowded room
and no one would notice.

I am doing all I can to
hold back the darkness,
but I can feel it creeping in
through the cracks in my skin.

I reach for love through the dark,
but love is far, far away from me,
and the deepest parts of me
weep in the language of lonely.

please, I just need someone to hold me.

my heart calls your name.
but you are too far away
to answer its call.

I'm starting to wonder
if you were ever
there at all.

I'm calling for you.
can you hear me through the static?
am I only a memory in your attic?
is there nothing left of us besides
a photo album collecting dust?

am I the only one who remembers *us?*

I wanna break free from
the ghost of your hands
tightening around me.

your memory is strangling me, and
I'm left dangling from your grip.
suffocated by your lips.

am I too broken to be fixed?

is it really art if I have to break my heart
into a million bite sized pieces to create it?
just to make it easier for people
to consume, digest, and understand?
would that not be considered
a massacre? a bloodbath?

I just want to be seen as I am.

little by little,
you took my heart
and broke it apart,
piece by brittle piece.

you were not a lover,
but a collector of miseries.

my heart is a collage,
a collection of souvenirs
from lovers I once held dear.
it's a locket worn around my neck,
a secret I am sworn to protect.

it's the only piece of you I have left.

they say you don't know what you have until you lose it.
in the same respect, you don't know how tight the noose is
until it's too late, and your heart is choking and *useless.*

I choke on the echo
your words left behind.
every night, in the dark,
yours hands, like ghosts,
crawl under my sheets
and remind me of the night
you took your time with me.
the night your translucent fingers
chased chills up my spine
and encased my heart in ice.

       official cause of death: *frostbite.*

every time I smell your cologne,
I am thrown into survival mode.
I claw at my chest, gasping for breath,
but I'm frozen like stone.

every time I see your ghost, *I choke.*

I'm running on empty.
all that remains of you are fumes,
wisps of someone I once knew.
a whispering mist of
someone I long to kiss.
my heart is now a host to
the ghost of the one I loved most.

I don't know how I'll ever let you go.

I know I can't go on like this—
clinging to you with white-knuckled fists
as you sink to the bottom of the chasm
that once housed us.

as the water weighs down on me and
the instinct to breathe increases exponentially,
I am faced with the impossible decision:
do I let you drag me down with you…

or do I let you go?

it's hard for me to fathom
moving on with your ghost in my way,
a phantom of all the things I wanted to say
hanging over me like a shadow—like a secret.
no one else can see you, *but I know you're there.*

I wear your memory *everywhere.*

I'd do anything to shake
the visceral ache in these limbs.
to eviscerate the pain that echoes
in the tangled throes that make up
this body, this heart, this home.

this skin is
haunted by the sins
of every ghost that has
ever passed through it.
my moans are their hymns.
my sobs, their worship.

> they say healing is worth it,
>   but *I don't think I have the courage.*

my heart is a hotel for ghosts.
it is the place where lost souls convene,
my heartbeat like a beacon
calling them home.

come home.

    come home.

        come home.

I spend my days
hauling my heartache
like an overstuffed suitcase.
filled to the brim, bursting at the seams.
hurting, it seems, incessantly.
          undeserving.
          indefinitely.
it weighs down on me like a boulder—
how much colder my world is without you in it.
how much older I am than the girl who lost you.

it's funny—the people that haunt you are often
the same people that taught you *ghosts aren't real.*
that *they're only shadows of the things we feel and can't say.*
things like, *I love you. I don't want to lose you this way.*
things like, *you are my everything, my every day.*

it's funny—those people—the *everything* people—
are often the same people that leave you with *nothing.*
with your heart in your hands—*nothing* left of it
but shredded, bloody, pulp that slips
through your fingers into a puddle on the floor,
and you slither down with it because *nothing* matters anymore.
curled up—*giving* up—when you would give *anything*
to feel something that isn't n~~othing~~umb.

so, I spend my days hauling my heartache,
because my pain is the only tangible proof
of how deeply I loved you.

haunt me, then,
until it doesn't hurt
to miss you like I do.

haunt me, then,
until I have the strength to
leave this bed you bound me to.

haunt me, then,
until there's nothing left
for me to do
but join you.

I'm the suffer in silence type,
which means I've forfeited my right
to scream about the night
that made me afraid
to turn out
the lights.

please don't turn out the lights.

once upon a time,
a little girl turned out the lights,
and the monster under her bed
whispered lies into her head:

nobody loves you, and
    you'd be better off dead.

the voices in my head have nothing to eat,
so, they feast on my insecurities.
they are not picky eaters;
they'll eat whichever one they
sink their sharpened teeth into first.
such insatiable thirst.

they could swallow each thought in one gulp,
but they would rather savor the pungent flavor
of my self-inflicted wounds.
they lick their lips, their fingertips,
savoring every last drop of crimson
trickling down their chin.
indulgent, greedy, always
needing more—*like you.*

luckily for them, there's plenty to go around.
they could come back for seconds, thirds,
fourths, and there'd be plenty of
vulnerabilities leftover.
scores and scores.

the voices in my head have nothing to eat.
they are rabid with hunger, *salivating.*
they are ravenous like wolves.
and, with teeth like thorns,
they swarm.

how to deal with anxiety:

1.) smother it with a pillow like you would a scream when everyone in the house is sleeping. *nobody can know you're still awake and agonizing over every breath you take.*

2.) starve it like a protestor on a hunger strike. *refuse to take another bite until it promises not to bite back.*

3.) ignore it like reoccurring chest pain or blinding headache. *no one would believe you, anyway.*

4.) submerge it in blood, liquor, tears, or sweat and hold it under until it takes its final breath. *do not resuscitate.*

5.) throw it in a body of water with cinderblocks chained to its ankles. let it sink to the bottom with a promise tucked between its teeth: *if you bury me now, I'll bring you down with me.*

my anxiety corrupts *everything* I touch.

it's always telling me *I'll never be enough*.

I've been broken beyond belief,
consumed by pain *beyond relief.*
lying in bed, gasping for breath,
is there any oxygen left?
are any of my atoms untouched
by the toxicity you call *love?*

     will I ever fucking be enough?

I've felt wrong
for so fucking long
that I don't know what it's like
or if I've ever even *felt* right.
misshapen and distorted,
mind and body contorted, twisted.

I don't know if *this* is my true form
or if I've permanently
shape-shifted.

anything is better than the way I feel right now.
like a disaster of epic proportions.
a mistake everyone regrets making in the end.
a bad memory everyone would rather forget.
anything is better than this.

> *will it ever get better than this?*

I thought if I laid you to rest,
I could finally catch my breath.
but here I remain, hidden away
and gasping beneath my shame.

the weight is far too heavy,
compressing my lungs.

how have I not suffered enough?

I locked my heart away
to keep it hidden—to keep it safe.
but it's spent so much time in isolation,
I've forgotten the combination.

and what was once a safe
became a lonely grave.

my heart is heavenbound.
heartstrings wound tightly,

I miss you nightly.

I have never tasted
grief like this before.
devouring my very core,
she swallows me whole
and begs me for more.

rivers of tears won't quell
her thirst, but my ocean eyes
can't help but   b u   r   s   t.

I miss you wholly.
    I miss you so much *it hurts*.

I talk to my pillow for one reason only:
the night is so dark, and I am *so lonely.*

there's nothing left for me to hold on to
but your scent in its thread count,
weaved between my sheets
where you used to sleep.

I bury myself in your side of the bed
and pray my weeping can bring you back to life.
is grief not a prayer in itself?
pleading with God for a resurrection,
a miracle, an undoing.

> *bring him back,*
>   *or take me with him.*

I was born in a grave,
   six feet beneath the girl

you begged me to be.

sometimes I feel like I was born at rock bottom.
I gasp awake from the dream—alive in the bedrock of grief.
bred of mud and soil, my lungs toil to breathe through the
dirt—the debilitating hurt of not knowing what I'm worth.

I'm clawing and scratching my way to the surface,
fingernails dirt-caked and bleeding, heart barely beating.
skin scraping the gravel, lungs chafing the scaffolds of
my protruding ribs, rubbed raw and screaming,
"you're better than this."

I'm better than this.

and so, I climb, my skinned knees and shattered dreams
dragging behind me like a shadow I can't shake,
desperate to break through the crust into a world
where maybe—just maybe—*I will finally be enough.*

sometimes I feel like I was born at rock bottom.
six feet underneath a tombstone that reads:
"here lies the burning girl, extinguished by her own flame.
what a shame, what a waste, but may she rest in peace."

someone resurrect me.

don't mind me—
not my dry hands,
cracked and letting all the light in.
photosynthesizing life—
as if that would work this time.

don't mind me—
not my bloodshot eyes,
glassy and weeping, openly grieving
the loss of everything that made me whole.
it'll take a miracle for me to let you go.

don't mind me—
not the earthquake in my chest
camouflaged as a heart shattered.
my sinus rhythm seismic—erratic—
will you stop being so damn dramatic?

don't mind me—
not me falling apart at the fault lines,
coming apart at the seams—*unravelling*—
ripping at the stitches keeping me together,
because it's pointless now that we're not—*together.*

~~so, don't mind me.~~
so, don't mend me.

my nerves are so fried
and my skin is so dry,
I pick and peel my nailbeds
until there's nothing left of them.
until my fingers are raw and bleeding,
and I'm helpless to stop ~~you from leaving~~.

we're all a little addicted to heartbreak,
searching for our next fix in the arms
of someone far too careless.

why are we so desperate
to blame someone else for
the pain we inflict on ourselves?

I need something to numb the pain.
so, I spend my days searching for ways
to silence the screaming in my veins,
to soothe my atoms that ache with longing.

as my heart grows weak beneath the strain
of having to beat on her own,
I stumble through the haze, the unknown,
feeling my way through the gray
to try and find my way home.

      on nights
         likc these,
            I feel so alone.

my heart is bleeding through its bandages.
pleading, pounding, beating hard
against the walls of my flesh.
crimson seeping between the crevices
of the dressing keeping it together.

mummified, it aches for a love that wasn't *mine*.
with one longing look in your direction,
I know my pain is *justified*.

my heart is like a broken window with
shards of glass snarling like teeth—
don't cut yourself on me
when you leave.

I'm the only one born to bleed for us.

when you crashed into me, *I could hardly breathe.*
an anvil on my chest, I still cannot accept
it was *you* who plunged your fist deep
inside and crushed my heart by the handful.

it's still hard for me to believe that
    your love could be too much for me to handle.

every time I see your face,
my heart finds another way to break.

the same way yours would *if you had one.*

your lips tasted like black lace
and a heart waiting to be broken.
I mourn the love we made
   before heartbreak came along
              and made fools out of us.

                    how could love be *not enough?*

your heart is a black hole.
carnivorous, corrupt.
swallowing everything
mine ever touched, ever loved.

all the love in the world could
never be enough to fill yours up.

you feel like a virus—*sickening.*
you slither like a snake—*venomous.*
you growl like an empty stomach—*gluttonous.*
like a virus—burning out and through every body you can sink
your teeth into.
like a snake—plunging your fangs into every creature that dare
falls into your trap.
like hunger—indiscriminate, filling yourself up with as many
women you can catch.

you ravenous, villainous, insatiable *man.*

my heart is guilt-riddled and ripped down the middle. torn apart by a reckless man and his malignant hands. in his eyes, my heart was the perfect prize—a sacrificial lamb *who never stood a chance.* in his eyes, her sacrifice put the "art" in "martyr"— his *pièce de résistance*—because she wouldn't—couldn't— *didn't*—**resist**—and it haunts her to this day; the part she played in her own demise. how she could've looked into his heartbreak eyes and fallen for his blatant lies. how? *how?* **how** could she let a murderer coax his way inside and hurt her? how could she not know he would take her by the throat and *never* let her go? she couldn't have known. *she couldn't have known.* you crippled her—*belittled* her—and now, she can't remember a time she ever felt whole, and she carries that emptiness with her everywhere she goes. *brittleness is all she knows.* she's falling apart the way you hoped she would from the start—piece by piece, slowly but surely *shattering.* you aren't around anymore to bear witness to the way she clamps handcuffs around her own wrists. imprisoned in the skin complicit in a crime she didn't commit, she is *desperate* for acquittal. the lone survivor of a foe formidable, *she* shouldn't pay the price for *your* sins— for *your* crimes inexplicable.

you wronged *her* in ways **unforgiveable.**

you wanted nothing less
than everything I had to give,
even if it wasn't yours to have and hold.
your greedy hands were unforgiving and cold,
your grip unrelenting. your love, twofold.
contingent on my surrender.
you were not a lover, but
a violent offender.

the night was fragile like glass.
like a bleeding heart in the palm of a malicious hand.
you held me like a grudge and broke me like a promise;
without regard or regret. with a white-knuckled fist.
with a hammer and chisel to the chest.

"stay still—I'm not finished yet."

-after Fall Out Boy, *"Hold Me Like a Grudge"*

I never wanted you to leave.
I only ever wanted you to love me
the way you love *yourself*.
to look at me the way you do *her*.
to hold me with the strength
that you hold a grudge.

you don't know what it means to *love*.
but when it comes to *want*,
you can never get enough.

I wake to the sound of *her* name on your dream-stricken lips.
they will *never* taste the same again. your kiss, tainted.

my love, *wasted.*

when I see you with her,
my stomach churns.

that should be *us*.

I loved you *first*.

without you to hold me down,
I am left to drift aimlessly,
floating, weightlessly.
without purpose.

I hope she was worth it.

I thought I knew you, but I didn't.
I didn't know that every night
after we turned out
the lights, you
dreamed
of *her*.

I didn't know that every time
you left, you weren't just
leaving the house.
you were
leaving
me.

I didn't know that every time
you told me you loved me,
you were only practicing.
only working up the
courage to look
past me and
into *her*.

her eyes,
   her heart,
      her soul.

I didn't know that
she was the one
for you.

I didn't know that
I was just a
substitute.

it kills me to know that
you are somewhere
out there loving
someone that
isn't *me*.

longing for you
anyway is *devastating*.

nothing will ever fill the void
loving you then *losing you*
left behind.

loving you has been the honor of a *lifetime*.
if only you could have stayed a part of *mine*.

you changed my life
in every possible way.

why couldn't you stay?

you've been gone
     for so many years.

          how have I not run out of tears?

I need something to do
that isn't constantly

missing you.

since you've been gone,
I've had a lot of time on my hands.
they long to be entwined with yours,
so, I keep them busy to keep them
from missing you.

it's the hardest thing I've ever had to do.

these poor hands
cannot stand
the empty space
you left between
their fingers.

craters.
  canyons.
        chasms.

this poor heart stalls.
                    seizes.
                        spasms.

    living without you is too hard
            for this poor body *to fathom.*

I find myself at a loss for words.
as a poet, I cannot describe
just how much *that hurts*.
to be bursting at the seams
and completely unable to scream.

how incredibly *tormenting*.

I am a poet.
how can I not know what to say?
how to correctly portray all the hurt churning
in the empty caverns of my chest,
burning a hole in my hollow, aching soul?
you collect discarded hearts like kindling,
strike the match, and let the wildfires of
melancholy catch and admire the way they burn.
some call it arson, but *you* call it *art*,
and you'd think that by now, I'd know
that where there's smoke, *there's a liar.*

I am a poet.
how can I not know how to
string together all my tangled thoughts
to paint an intricate picture of all this pain?
a self-portrait of my mangled bones bleeding
in the hands of all the ghosts that broke me:
grotesque. baroque. my misery bespoke,
custom-made to fit into the mold you shaped
like a girl you could have your way with.
desperate to make me fit, you fractured me into a million
tiny pieces, dropped—shattered—split—scattered me
until all that remained were echoes and traces,
phantoms of what I could've been, but
the truth of the matter is, I can't be *her.*
I will *never* be her—I am my *own* kind of disaster.

I am a poet.
how can I not know how to convey it?
how to phrase it, to make it make sense
when I can't even comprehend it myself?
my mind—*betrayed*—my heart—*flayed*
and spilling out of my pores in waves
impossible to ignore but *ignored all the same.*
invisible to the naked eye but *prominent in mine.*
if only someone—*anyone*—would dare to look deeper.
could anyone bear to see the real her?

I am a poet.
why am I holding back the truth?
why am I so afraid of the world discovering the real *you?*
of shining a light on the torment you put me through
and the strength it took me to survive you?
why am I so afraid of being the one to blame
when *you* are the one who turned on *me?*
the one who sharpened my shame into a knife
and used it against me—*the perfect crime.*
you plunged it heart-deep, my spine its sheath,
and made a home for yourself in porous bones.
even when I'm alone, *I'm not,* because even though
you are long gone, *your memory still holds on.*

I am a *poet.*
how have I become so fluent in silence?
so comfortable in this quiet charade that
your ghost hasn't overstayed its welcome?
it has—*you have*—and I don't know how to kick you out.
how to exorcise—evict—eradicate—*eliminate*
you from the molecules that store memory.
from the heinous muscle you claimed as your own,
the same traitorous one that still loves you to the bone.
they say the body keeps the score, *and you hold the highest.*
they say that love is war, and yours was *so violent*—
bloody and brutal. abhorrent and feudal.
my judgment—*skewed*—your ambition—*shameless*—
but I know *I am not blameless in this.*
my hands, bloodstained like yours.
my conscience, shredded and torn,
you made me wish I was never born.

I am a poet.
I know better than most
that secrets are safest kept inside,
hidden deep between the lines of the poems I write.
confessions penned in invisible ink:
how could I let you do this to me?

your shadow casts an eerie haze across each poem,
dangles, sways from every stanza like a noose
like you always knew *I would hang myself on you.*

but how is it that the cavity of your absence
is larger than your presence ever was?
a gaping wound, a bottomless hole
in which the laws of gravity do not apply.
your exodus ripped open a chasm, an endless void
in which my secrets are a swirling mass of screams,
but as they reach my mouth, become timid whispers.
ragged gasps. how could I let you take me— *b r e a k me* —
and leave me like that?

I am a poet…
but you knew that.
you knew all it would take was a single, simple heartbreak,
and you would be immortalized in rhyme *forever.*
I may be a disaster, but you… you are a *cancer.*
malignant. lethal. a pestilence that won't rest
until you've eaten everything in your path.
vicious and insatiable. certain and *inescapable.*

I am a disaster,
but *you* are a *massacre.*
cruel, callous, and ruthless.

I knew resisting you was *useless.*

I don't know why
    I hold on to you so tight
            when you always *fight back.*

you struggle in my grip,
    blindly swinging your fists.
            why do you *always resist?*

        I just want
            you to love me
                like you once did.

my memories are
blurry and tangled,
my heart twisted
and mangled.

but my feelings are
so raw and tangible,
physically palpable.

you could slice them
mid-air with a knife—
all these feelings that have
no way to escape.

     I have
        no proof—
              only pain.

my memories, they disagree.
  time, it seems, has had its way with me.

I pick fights with my memories
of nights long passed, not knowing
how long I will last, if at all.

I pick fights with my memories.
I'm frightened of them all.

I don't want to think of you anymore.
I pick at the memories of us until
my heart is frayed and sore,
my muscles ache, and
my soul contorts
with guilt and
shame.

if this
  is what it
     means to love you,

          I don't want to anymore.

I don't love you anymore.
and I am growing tired of waiting
for your ghost to gather its things and cross over.

my heart is not your home.
   my hands are not yours to hold.

you were a guest here, passing through
on your way to someone new, and I never
should've let you stay in my guest room.

   years have passed,
      and it still smells like you.

I lock the door and hide the key somewhere
I can't reach so, the next time you knock,
I won't have a place for you to stay, because

      I don't love you anymore.
         not the way I did before.

falling out of love
with you was a silent battle.

a war waged behind closed doors,
out of sight of wandering eyes.

I bleed for us. weep for us.
because you will *never* be mine.

I'm learning to be fine with that:
unloving someone who will
never love me back.

you fled on the cusp of daybreak,
as the dream-stricken sky
burst into color
all for us.

you kept your face, your gaze
on the ground beneath
your retreating feet,
never looking up at
the composition I
painted just
for us.

you once said, *love is blind,* and you were right.
you looked at me, eyeless, and said
you could never love someone
so black and white, oblivious
to the fact that

I was the only color in your life.

215

I wish I could say that
I have moved on, and believe it.

I wish. *I will.*

I wish I could say that without you,
I'm better off, and believe it.

I wish. *I will.*

I wish I could say that
I don't love you anymore, and believe it.

I wish. *I will.*

I wish I could say that
I don't need you anymore… and believe it.

I wish. *I will.*

one of these days
when you look my way,
I won't be looking back at you.
I will finally be moving on
like I should've been
all along.

take what you want from me and *leave.*
because the sooner you go,
the sooner I will see

I am better off alone.

I know exactly what you want:
someone who will do *that*.
whatever you want, whatever you ask
with no second guessing, no holding back.
you want someone who will worship at your feet,
but I will *never* be the kind of girl
who loves on her knees.

I am, and have always been,
the kind of girl who loves
long after love *leaves*.

I will never beg you to stay,
but I will always,
         always,
                always love you, anyway.

I have so much left to say to you.
things like, "I love you, but I deserve better."
things like, "I know in your own way,
you loved me more than words could ever say,
but you could've at least *tried*."

things like, "I loved you blindly,
and now I miss you nightly,
but never enough to unmake all this progress,
to thwart this healing process."
things like, "I know I'm not perfect,
but *I know I am worth it*."

I have so much left to say to you.
so much more than could ever be said
within the confines of a simple phrase.

> *I love you* can't hold a candle
> to the inferno we set ablaze,

> but the time has come
> *to extinguish the flames.*

I want you to be happier
than you ever were
when we were together.

I'm no fool—I know I am
a far from perfect lover, and
I don't want you to lose sleep
over someone so incomplete.

so, go—find a lover who knows
how to make broken things whole.
find someone who can stoke
the smoldering embers of your soul
into an eternal flame that lights
your way to happiness.

I want us *both* to find love like that.
so, go—and don't ever look back.

I know I won't.

there are very few things in life that I know for certain.

one:
one day, you will wake,
rip open your bedroom curtains,
the sun will cast an ethereal glow
on your empty bed,
and you will long for me
to appear between the sheets.
you will ache for the ghost of me,
but I will be *far* out of reach.

two:
too much time has passed.
every moment I ever spent waiting
for an answer, a reason, was wasted.
my every effort to hold you closer
only widened the rift,
only deepened the chasm,
and we can *never* bridge that gap.
you took years of my life
and oceans of my love
I will *never* get back.
I've since learned how to accept that.

three:
is a crowd.
there was not enough room
in our story for you, me, and *her*.
so, I saw myself out.

I hope she was worth it.

things I never got to mention:
a collection of afterthoughts.

I never liked the way you looked at me.
like I was a sight to behold, someone to be told,
"you're beautiful the way you are—*underneath me.*"

I never liked being at your every beck and call,
but whenever I needed you, you were nowhere
to be found—*nowhere at all.*

I never liked being the only one you'd call
in the middle of night, just so you could talk
about someone else—*the very one I warned you about.*

I never liked how you seemed happier without
me in your life. I grew accustomed to life without *you,*
but it took years' worth of sleepless nights,
whereas it only took you *one.*

I've never liked not knowing if you miss me.
if you ever wake up in the middle of the night
and reach for your phone to call me while she is
sound asleep beside you—*I'd like that.*

to wake up at three a.m. to your name on my caller ID.
for my love to wake up beside me and ask, "Who is that?"
for me to roll my eyes, send you to voicemail,
kiss him goodnight, and say,

"Nobody."

you don't read my poems anymore.

so, I must update you:

I've written six books—so far—and, yes, that's *you* nestled between the lines. weaved into their binding. glued into their spines. I have two more in the works, and rest assured, you'll find strands of your hair knotted in the letters that tie each verse together. I don't know which of the two of us has it worse—the curse, or *the* cursed.

my drink of choice is wine now, but I'm not drinking to forget anymore. *that's what writing poetry is for.* without it, I can't otherwise admit that I still taste you on the lips of every bottle begging to be consumed—*begging, like you.* it recently crossed my mind that *I haven't been sober since that night you came over.* and maybe it's time to dry myself out—dry *you* out—and maybe, just maybe, it will starve my tongue long enough to forget the way yours felt against my teeth.

maybe that's why I can't let you go—once I put the bottle down, I'll know the truth: that the blame isn't on me. *it's all on you.* it will take some getting used to; not living with that shame that tethers me to you. I never realized how heavy the burden of truth was until it all came crashing down on me. all of your lies are so deeply woven into my bones—so entangled in my genomes—I hardly know who I am beyond the broken. beyond the pain. *I wonder if it matters, anyway.*

but then, I remember I never have to worry about what you think—*ever again.* the only thing that matters is *I am happier now than I've ever been.*

and that's not on you—*that's all on me.*

-after Maria Giesbrecht

some nights are eerily quiet.
there's nothing but the sound of
my heartbeat in my ears and
blood rushing through my veins
to reassure me that I'm alive.
that I survived you.

some nights, there's nothing but
the sound of my ragged breath
and the churning in my stomach
cutting through the darkness to
remind me I was only dreaming.
you are nothing but a memory.

some nights, the silence swallows me.
the emptiness engulfs me, endless
and revolting as I vividly recall
the way you used to hold me.
so tightly. *so unholy.*

but some nights, I don't mind the silence.
I find myself there, better off somewhere
that isn't where you left me.
I find I am beautiful in the silence
like I could never be in your presence.

in that silence, *I've found peace.*

other titles by Jenna:

Flames Speak
Love Like a Storm
Carnage: poems for the haunted
The Art of Starving
Bone Weaving

Available on Amazon and Etsy.

about the poet

Jenna Malin is self-published out of St. Louis, Missouri.
Kissing Catastrophe is her sixth collection of poetry.

Visit her online at   *jennasdilemmas.net*

Threads: @poems.by.jenna

Instagram: @poems.by.jenna

TikTok: @jennasdilemmas

Order signed copies of her books at   *jennasdilemmas.etsy.com*